Pulling off the Edge

By: Ashley Morgan

It's raining hard outside. There are rows of corn for miles, and I think I left my record player outside. I had some clothes out there, but it's too late to find them in the mud.

It's dark now too. The winds are picking up. I guess my boys are already inside. I think my husband is still out here in this field with his friend. I can't see them now.

I just have a pressing need to pack up and get going.

The boys are playing down the hallway. My stuff is scattered everywhere. How did I get so scattered? Clothes are everywhere. Mom gave me her hand-me-downs and a few clothes. I didn't need them, but maybe it's just nice to have something kinda new.

I look out of the window. It's square; the corn is swaying hard, and the rains have made a muddy bathtub out of the field.

I call for my boys. I tell them it's time to go.

I run to the bathroom still picking up clothing that's strewn across the floor. I sit down and push the door shut. I reach down for toilet paper, and the door pops open. In survivor -whiplash-instinct, I yell, "No! Out!" and, I push the door shut.

I see mom's head pop in the door. I let off my strength.

I'm sitting there half-dressed, clothes hanging out of my suitcase and she insists on coming in *now*. I give up being covered up, and I look up.

She stands there like a yellow paper mache' doll. Three red buttons down her chest. She is spattered in blood. She yells in a whispered vent of anger, "Fuckin' Nigger*s!"

I wake up sweating.

Just as long as we're together

Writing this is hard. As you will see I am doing all I can to give myself permission to share these things, but it's a battle.

It's a battle of guilt. It's a battle of betrayal. It's a battle that I feel inside I'm still hiding. Though names are changed, details are adjusted, I still hide like a child, well-past the child years.

She said when I was born, it was "You and I against the world." She didn't feel like anything would defeat us- -just as long as we were together.

But, over time, things changed. And, the more I tried to pull away, the more she stuck to me, and the more I felt pulled me down- -especially when I tried to pull away.

If I tried to voice what I needed, my feelings were not acknowledged. Even when she asked about my plans, the question was less about *my* answer and more about what she wanted from me.

I learned that most of the time what she wanted from me was affection and admiration. Most of the time, it was more than I had in me to give.

Last week, my therapist said it was time to go "no contact" with my mom. This sounded like an insane suggestion.

I asked, "But, then, what about her?"

He said, "Exactly."

Hopeful

Things were a bit easier when she lived three states away. When she moved back to my town- -the dream town, her expectations grew, and the space I needed to grow my *own* way shrank a little more every single day.

It felt like my walls were closing in.

Bubbles

Then, slowly, this is when things started to bubble toward the surface.

At first, I was excited- -hopeful. But within a year's time, I felt like I couldn't breathe.

When my therapist recommended that I start reading books about "Borderline Personality disorder," everything started to come together.

After 40 years of feeling like a lost child, I suddenly realized everything was not *my* fault. And, like a child, even at the age of 40, I spent a lot of time hiding.

I found myself stuffing my car in my garage so she won't know I am home, so she won't *just* drop by.

The therapist, my fourth one since she moved here, suggested I finally build a boundary. He suggested that I go 'no contact,' at least for a little while.

Though, he made it sound easier, the no-contact thing is actually tricky. I can be busy, but now, it's summertime and well, she will say all of my excuses should fade.

My former therapist told me what to do.

She said, "Well, we always stay busy. Busy never stops."

Easier said than done.

Mom called last week, and asked if she could take my oldest, Jason, for a few weeks as she drove down the East coast. I made up busy words. In fact, we *do* have things on the calendar. And, I got off of the phone.

My son seemed excited about the venture. But, then, after I put down the phone, I told him I didn't think it was a great idea.

I said, "Don't you remember the last time you were there? She said if you didn't choose your shoes quickly, she would 'beat the hell out of you.'

And, you came home so sad and down for nearly two days. I just can't send you back to that."

My son just looked down and then away in silence.

It was hard to tell him these things. But, I also wanted to protect him.

My own choices

I remember when I told her I was having my second child. She got mad at me.

Mom said, 'Well, what about Jason?'

Then, she grew to love my second child as her 'favorite.'

And, when I didn't talk to her first about my third child, she was furious with me when I told her we were expecting Ray.

She felt like I *should* wait three to five years between each child. I think she must have also felt rejected or abandoned in some way. Maybe she worried I wouldn't have as much time for her. Maybe she felt left out. Maybe she just had other issues I'll never understand.

When I had my first, she cheered, bought me clothes; she was there for nearly every event. When I was expecting my second, it was a different world.

I remember nearly losing the second child. It was a difficult time. But, within a few weeks, I was back at work trying to find a way through it all, without her support.

When I was finally expecting my second child, and things seemed okay, I was often feeling as if I was going to be sick often. But, if I mentioned it, it was as if I was asking for too much attention. I would wait and wait and wait to get her permission for the things that I needed or the things the baby was telling me he needed.

Things hadn't changed much since I had had my first child. When it was time to breastfeed my first born, she thought it was gross. She made me wait and wait to feed him because it was inconvenient.

I knew it was time. I felt it was time. He was squirming like it was *past* time. Moms just kind-of know this. We didn't have ten minutes to wait before Jason would cry. I waited another ten, and finally fed him. But, it was very uncomfortable as I look back and realize, even then, I was putting her needs above my own and above my child's.

I was always worried about her. Looking back, it's symbolic that I struggled for permission to feed my child. He had picked an inconvenient time to be hungry. I've done that before too.

I remember expecting my second child and being hungry in Target. I was pushing her over-filled basket, and my 15-year-old sister wanted to ride on the cart. I said, "I can't push this cart."

Having miscarried twice before, I was especially careful not to overload myself. But, she seemed to have forgotten those two years and how hard they were on me when she said, 'Push the cart.'

I am thirty something. And, it's still a fight. But, I rebelled. I stopped for a Snickers bar.

Mom laughed and scoffed, 'Well, you *ate* through the Target trip.'

I was needing, suddenly, to take care of someone else besides her. I didn't want her to be angry. I didn't want to pose a problem. I didn't *need* the attention. But, I also needed not to throw up.

The patterns seem to be the same, whether shopping, or waiting, or not being able to wait. It's interesting when I stop to consider the patterns in the details even many years later. If I look back, I feel empowered with the patterns, and I feel less like a child stuck in a hole.

I remembered then, wandering through Target with her again that day, when I had to stop to nurse Jason. And he was about to just lose it.

She said, 'Ten more minutes.'

I said, 'We don't *have* ten more minutes.' And, my son cried as I waited for her and finally, in the car, I did the most bold thing ever and nursed him in the car while she put away the groceries. The fumes from the car were awful, but her looking at me doing "that thing" was even harder than not being able to breathe.

She hated the idea of me nursing. She felt like it was unnecessary when a bottle worked just fine. I realize too that she probably wanted to be able to feed my children as well. She was left out of the loop. I almost felt like apologizing that nursing was working. I didn't expect it to work, but it did.

We went out to dinner once and he cried and she said in an emergency tone, 'What are you going to *do*? *Run* to the bathroom!'

I felt her panic, and when she panicked, I became a child all over again trying to appease her.

By the third and final child, I had one of those fancy breastfeeding covers, and worried a lot less. Or, I just went to the car - -not out of embarrassment, but mainly to be alone. It was one less thing on the table at the time - -one less stress on my shoulders.

We were different people

But, I couldn't always do things her way. I didn't marry three times. I didn't have a child with each dad. I didn't start my family at the age of 20. I was older, with a career, and the first person in our household with a college degree. I had accomplished a lot. And, yet, it didn't seem like enough, to her, for me to make my own decisions.

It still seems odd that she hung up the phone when I told her I was expecting my third child. It wasn't a case for celebration, but a case for her to somehow feel abandoned and angry.

I was finding my own way, I was already in my mid—
thirties with fertility and miscarriage stories. I couldn't wait nine and
22 years between each child like she did.

See, there's me, even now, rationalizing a decision, as an
adult, that I am allowed to make. Yes, I am angry. Most of all, it is an
angry hurt. I don't like to be angry at anyone. And it's especially
difficult when my feelings don't seem to matter.

When I finally got through those terrible three months, I
told her I was expecting Ray and, as a gift, so she wouldn't have to
worry, I told her when the doctor said everything was okay, that I was
expecting Ray. There, I was again, trying to make things better for
her. I told her about the pregnancy once I had gone through the tough
part-- alone. In a time when I could have used support, I chose,
instead, to support her and her feelings over my own.

She hung up on me. I was not celebrated by having a
healthy pregnancy after two miscarriages and a year of infertility
treatments, but scolded for not waiting on her green light.

By not making her first, I had become her last.

You're not mine

She was always disowning me. She says, if I do this or that,
I'm 'not her daughter.' It's like I get to be emotionally close to her for
a time, and then I get pushed away.

My first decision

I decided to marry the guy I dated for three years, and after a year of engagement and finishing my college degree; she disowned me. She said if I went through with the marriage, I wasn't 'her daughter.'

And then, the day of the wedding, she was late. She said she didn't want to bring my dress. She wanted to 'keep driving to Fairhope.' I had been to her house the night before to steam the dress. My oldest friend was there to help me as we struggled to steam the dress with a neighbor's gear. I was leaving my dress in her hands hoping she'd participate in some way. I learned later that was a bad idea.

And, I was left to think to myself, two hours before my wedding, whose dress could I borrow and who was *about* my size. I began to plan a backup plan. One of my bridesmaids had a sister *about* my size. And, I think I could fit into her dress. It may not have been *my* style, but it was an option. And, her house was 15 minutes away. And, she was invited to the wedding, so that would be the plan.

Mom, eventually, brought the dress- -the one I had her pick out with me together. I, all along, was trying to find something her and I could do together. I wanted the mother daughter bond that comes when picking out that dream wedding dress. It felt more like a

Texan shoveling snow for the first time. We rushed a bit that day because she had to bring my two-year-old sister with her while we went dress shopping. I really wanted her to *want* to be there with me to pick out the dress. But, she didn't feel it.

She didn't feel it for my rehearsal dinner either. She didn't come. She explained, 'You know I have your sister."

We picked the dress. I bought it. $347. It took me three months to pay it out. Even paying for the dress was a struggle, but I did it.

I thought to myself, just about six months ago, my grandmother gave me her entire fortune when she passed away- -$20k and her home in Virginia. When that happened, mom was so outraged, she immediately made me sign it over to her, and she split it with my aunt. My aunt got the house built in the early 1900s, and my mom took most of the cash. She gave me back $3k and said, 'That will make one Hell of a nice wedding!'

I had carefully budgeted the catering, the dress, the hall, the guests, and every single dime for 90 people. It didn't go as far as she said it would. But, three months later, I had a dress. And, I didn't have the money to have it hemmed. I just thought, I'll wear higher heels. Bad idea.

And, looking back, if I spent $300 on a dress, another $50 to have it hemmed, is nothing. Mom scolded me, she said, 'It was a waste!'

So, I wore the dress as it was, about an inch too long. Looking back, it wouldn't have been a waste at all. It was *my* day, and it would have been okay to feel perfect on my day.

Before the wedding words

She eventually brought the dress to the chapel.

The dressing room was a mess of bobby pins and stockings. The other bridesmaids were milling about and helping where they could.

There was a bridesmaid in the bathroom adjoined to the dressing room at the back of the chapel. I think my mom thought I was alone. Mom said, 'If he EVER does anything to hurt you. I will KILL him.'

I said something like 'Okay' and used that as an inner blessing and substitute for the traditional mother/daughter-wedding-day chat.

Wedding

My dad was on his best behavior. He was wearing a suit, unusual for him, and he and my mom managed, after being divorced for 20 years, to walk me down the aisle together. I figured it was a fair idea. My grandmother, the woman I spent so much time with when mom was away that I literally still have some of her habits, couldn't be there, so, I guess, my parents should walk me down the aisle. I was hopeful this would be a symbol for our future times with our future children, one day. We'd all just get a long. I laugh now looking back at my constant optimism.

Mom said, angrily, 'You didn't tell me WE were walking down the aisle together!!'

Her hot pink flowered as she called it 'so *not* mother of the bride' miniskirt told another story. My father kissed me on the cheek, and left me at the front. I believe it was the first time he'd ever kissed me. I don't know if I'd ever seen this side of him before.

My mother grabbed my father's youngest son. He was about six at the time. She held him like her teddy bear. Later, he told me he wondered. 'Who is this lady grabbing me and why am I in her lap?'

I walked down the aisle of wooden pews and smiled at my grandfather, my cousins and even a first love.

We then spent time taking pictures along dripless candles flagged in floors in plastic Saran wrap which made the pictures.

We piled into the hall, and I guess the gods knew best because the ceremony was cut short. The storm knocked out the power.

We ate and then said our brief hellos, had a short dance, one toast, a wedding cake war and we left with bubbles serenading our drive out in the rain.

I wasn't able to dance with my dad. Perhaps it was heaven's blessing. I have no idea how mom would have reacted to that notion.

I'm sorry. Not sorry

It's not that I don't love her.

She just loves me too much. Or, she just loves me too much in a way where I feel like I am drowning and my needs don't matter.

The therapist said it is something called "enmeshment." She feels that I am an extension of herself. Whatever happens to me also happens to her.

And she never learned to let go of that - -part of me as a part of herself.

And, in a sense, she lives through me and wants to control me to save herself. She fears abandonment. She fears me not needing her. She fears what she can't control. She fears the loss of herself.

And, I've always sort of been loyal to that feeling- -until now. And, if I got too close to someone, she'd make an end of it.

When I dated Dilliard- -my first love in the summer of my 8th grade year, she told his mom she didn't want us to date and then, I was no longer dating Dilliard. It was that simple. The doors were shut. It was like him and and I were walking up this hill together, and we were dragged down like rag dolls. It hurt for a long time.

When I was dating Bryce, in my sophomore year, I broke it off before it could hurt. She was satisfied for a moment or two, but then, she'd always want another act of sacrificial devotion.

When Kimble broke up with me my junior year, she gave me a high five. She was delighted that I was free because she didn't like the guy. I also remember him saying he wasn't sure he wanted to date me because my mom was hard to deal with. That was one of those relationships when I truly became whoever the guy wanted me to be- -a pattern I had until my early twenties.

Moods

And, because mom was hard to deal with, I was a bit more insecure than I needed to be. My security depended on her happiness despite her constant swiftly-changing moods.

At first, they'd be attracted to my tough exterior and then, my heart would cave in and then they'd own me, and then lose interest. I didn't know how to be me- -I didn't know who I was outside of her.

I worried about things becoming black and white all of the time. Not knowing a life when relationships were constantly changing, I was always expecting to be dropped.

For mom didn't have strong boundaries, when it came to asking questions that were way, way too personal. And, the way she loved me was my *only* example at the time. She being a single mom, and my dad being around every now and then, it wasn't long before I thought that might be the only way to love and to be loved. Naturally my friendships for the next twenty years were a bit fucked up.

Boundaries

When Jason was being incubated, she reached inside the top part of my jeans, and grabbed at my stomach without warning.

I'll never forget. We were laying in bed, and I was napping. I was being pumped full of progesterone to keep the pregnancy going. And she said, at about 18 weeks I'd start to feel the baby move 'Like bubbles! You will feel them.'

I remember shrinking back at her sudden grip into my private world. For that moment, it felt like she was trying to own that too.

I didn't feel him move until at least 22 weeks. But at the age of 28, I felt immobilized and powerless when she grabbed me in that way.

Perhaps, that's why I didn't have her come to my baby's birth. I knew if I was in pain, I knew if I was worried, my instincts would be to comfort her over myself. And, I knew, in a time of birth, I'd need to be selfish- -not for just me, but also for the baby.

Boxing ring or birthing day?

The day Jason was born, she went nuts. She was pacing all night she said and almost had "a heart attack." She was in distress. It took her hours to get to the hospital. She knew I was in labor for 16 hours, and she was only 45 minutes away. But, she was waiting for a friend to come with her.

When she got there, she was angry because my mother-in-law had gotten there first. And the MIL, the felon, who lived five hours away, was sitting in a chair facing the door of the hospital room.

The MIL looked up, and saw my mom and must have given her an "I got here first" look because my mom went nuts immediately.

Mom yelled, 'Clear the room! I want to talk to my baby. My baby had a baby!'

And, she jumped into bed with me.

Now, I was tied up to cords and swollen and stitched up. I was a mess. I was cut up and well, a third-degree tear. I had had the Pitocin pumped up so high, and was in labor for nearly 22 hours. I was also exhausted and a day-old mom. I later realized I was also suffering from PPD.

Mom squished me, and then got up quickly and grabbed Jason. She smiled with her girlfriend, and said her friend took too long.

We had time for one picture before my MIL walked back into the room. MIL said with a huff, 'You didn't have to be SO rude. You could have been more polite!'

Mom put the baby down, and suddenly had two free hands. She used them to grab my MIL's neck, and my MIL didn't back down. My FIL stood there coldly without motion. My husband called for security. I lay there numb.

And mom disappeared, and we don't see her again for three months. She said as long as my MIL is in the picture, she didn't want to be in the picture. My MIL, a former felon, has a past that my mom has spent hours looking up at the local newspaper morgue. It had been 25 years. That's not the best story either, but this was a new beginning, well, I *was* hopeful.

It's a baby. It's a birthday now covered in drama.

But, "He *said* it was okay."

Perhaps it was always easier not to feel anything than to say what I was feeling.

I spoke up once when I was 14. I was staying with my dad that weekend. I had season passes to the local rollercoaster park. My dad said I could go.

Mom said 'No' over the phone.

Dad said, 'Go.'

So, I went with my oldest friend. We had a blast.

When mom picked me up from dad's house fuming; she looked me straight in the eyes and with her right hand slapped me hard.

The "element of surprise" was strong that day.

She was puffing like a dragon.

Which way to turn

Going between households makes life weird. Dad said one thing. Mom said another. And, they were always giddy to put me in-between. I always felt like I was the rope in a tug-of-war match.

Dad would say I could, and mom would say no. Dad would pay for camp, and I was afraid to go, so mom nurtured the fear, and I didn't *have* to go. Things were always up and down there too.

When I was sixteen, my dad let me date. I was 15 actually, and I was helping out at his boat store. So with my friends, we'd pile into the car, we'd go to the movies, we'd go to the park. We were just silly kids.

One phone call, one of my dad's teen-faced employees said I was 'with Bryce.'

She picked me up right away. She took me out to a fancy lunch and looked me straight in the eyes, she asked, 'Do I need to put you on the pill?'

I didn't know what to say. I looked down and up again. I said, 'No.'

And I didn't understand what she was thinking or saying. I just went to the movies with my friends. I wasn't having sex at 15.

Looking back, I see she was reflecting upon her own life choices and not mine. And, it was unfair. She didn't know me.

She didn't know me

Flash forward 20 years. I am dancing. I am happy. I am free.

Later she tells me in a text that seeing me dance didn't seem right.

She said, "I don't know *that* girl."

It's 20 years later. And, I am dancing in the front row of my favorite musician's graces. When I see him play- -him and his band, I'm just free. This is as wild as I get. Something about his music makes me let go like I've never done before.

My mom was in the audience. She knew the opening singer, and happened to be there. She texted me telling me that I might know the main musician. I said, yes and the location.

I was wearing a self-made fan t-shirt. I was *that* kind of fan dork at this point in time. I walk over and said hello. I was kind. I was cheerful. But, I was also independent. Perhaps, too much so.

A few weeks later, she said I was a 'stranger.' She said she 'Didn't know the girl she saw that evening.' She was unhappy with my actions that night because she'd never seen that side of me before.

Letting loose and being vulnerable is not something I do very often. I have to feel safe.

Growing up I didn't always feel that way.

In the car, she used to make me dance to the Stones. She'd say, "Come on now! Be silly with me . . . oh you're no fun!"

But the truth is, I couldn't be her friend. I felt more like the adult in the relationship and letting go of that was completely confusing.

Making My Own Self

I remember in college, I was active in the Baptist student union. It was my safe place. I don't know why, but going to church alone, like theatre arts classes, became my safe place. At church I was accepted mostly for who I was. In theatre arts classes, I could be *anyone* I wanted. My youth pastors and theatre arts teachers always nurtured me in ways I didn't know existed. I found myself sometimes lost between those two worlds- -home and other people's normal.

Upon taking my friend Pete to the union to serve at yet another Christian conference- -one that I had already planned to attend- -suitcase in the trunk and ready to go.

She yelled, "You've gotta QUIT this Baptist CRAP!"

And, feeling squished, feeling alone, I dropped Pete off and came home. My bags were actually packed and ready to go, but I stayed home. I spent the entire weekend in my room putting a puzzle together and listening to Jennifer Knapp. I couldn't be what she wanted me to be, and when I tried, I just wasn't happy.

She crept into my room to ask if I wanted to come out with her.

I kept my head down and finished my puzzle.

I realized I needed that Baptist "crap" a great deal.

In the very place I sat putting the puzzle together is the very place she threw a hanger at my face just a few months before. I guess I had asked for too much. I had asked to stay out past 12 because I was 21, and I was in college.

I had missed the last 15 minutes of a movie because I had to be home by midnight. I remember using my quarters to use the payphone outside. I was asking for fifteen extra minutes.

She said it was inconvenient for me to stay out because she had to work; she stayed up until I got home and she "had to worry" about me. I paused and then spoke up. I said, "What about what *I* want?"

She paused too-- just long enough to throw a wire hanger at my face.

So, it's always been that way. It's always been punch and cover- -daggers and sharp words. Slamming doors. Conflicts are managed by slamming down phones and hangups - -hangups that don't go away.

Reaching out for help

I had heard that going to counseling could be helpful here, but the thought of it was terrifying. I began to consider it as perhaps a helpful adventure. I figured it couldn't hurt.

When I walked into the therapist's office, I realized I had Googled the wrong person. She wasn't wearing a turban, which was a relief. She *did* have a couch. She *did* have a clock. She did have tissues just within my grasp. She did have a big black chair facing me.

And, walking in, it felt like I was in the principal's office.

I thought, I am paying a *stranger* to hear my story. That just seemed dumb from the beginning. She is being paid to be my friend for an hour. That's just weird.

She immediately took my payment. Then, after signing $25 and my insurance info away, she exhaled and looked straight at me. It felt cold. Direct. Clinical.

She looked right at me and asked, "So why are we here today?" I thought about my feet beneath the floor. And, I began to just start crying.

I started to heave and wail. And, to think that I was crying in front of someone that just knew my name and my insurance company made it all worse.

I said, whimpering, "My mom is a (lengthy pause) bully."

I felt terrible because it felt like an act of betrayal.

I felt scared because if she knew what I was saying aloud, she'd come down hard on me. She'd either hit me with a hanger or slap me with her "element of surprise."

She'd then go onto call all of her esteemed friends, my brother, my sister, my step-dad and everyone else I loved, and tell them how terrible I was so that they'd disown me too.

Her tornado would wipe me non-existent.

This was the first time I was talking about my feelings. This was the first time I had acknowledged that they may matter, and this was the first time that I started to see myself as a whole person and not just a shadow.

The therapist said, "But, you aren't that child anymore. You don't have to be in *that* place."

I defended, "Yes, but she rages, and then it's me cowering in a corner with my head between my knees and my hands over my head. I am a dog with my head on the floor while she makes me sniff my mistakes."

She retorted, "But, you don't *have* to be. You are not 15 anymore. You have the power to walk away, the power to set boundaries, the power to mark your own terms."

It was like learning a new language. It was like looking behind the curtain and realizing it was okay to belong there.

Young people

I see young people today traveling across the world to study abroad. And, I wonder how their parents let them go. I remember asking one of my student's parents that question. The father just said simply, "It was a good opportunity for her."

It was the most unselfish response.

The Face of Love

The face of love changes. I struggle with what is real.

In fact, if I don't hear back from a friend, I assume we are no longer friends. Just like how my mom treats me, I assume if I made her unhappy, then, our relationship is sawed off.

This really makes relationships difficult. I have to tell myself that my friend is busy. I have to tell myself it's not something I did. It probably has nothing to do with me. And, it's not always my fault.

When the lady behind me at the concert wrapped her fingers around the lady's neck pushing her, going back into fifteen wasn't what I had planned.

The woman, who had friended me, who had looped her arm into mine, was now, in a blink, holding the girl behind me in a choke hold. Just like that. I blinked, and my mom was standing right beside me in this new person. A second ago, it was her and I against the crowd, and I blinked and the story changed.

I looked up, phoned a friend, and hopped the fence. Trying to calm down, I realized I was shaking, cold nerves, mistaken and lost. I told myself over and over to breathe.

It wasn't always that bad. I still feel bad writing this.

Now, it's not like it was THAT bad. I mean she didn't beat me. She just emotionally disabled me.

And, I stopped asking for what I needed.

Therapist number two said that people in my situations often learn to live in really bad situations. So, bad situations become the norm. And, I just learned to accept bad truths. And, in fact, I might look for bad situations because they are my normal.

Now, that's a lot to digest.

So how do I know what is *normal*? And, how do I get used to *easy or easier*?

I found I make myself as busy as possible. I take on many little jobs. I work longer hours. I don't give myself time to think. I don't give myself time to *feel*.

I am an octopus woman with many arms in the air

In the movie (*Anywhere But Here*) the closing remarks state, "When mom dies, the world will be flat," I agree with those words.

And, I am not sure what to do with "flat."

The therapist said that my mother needs me more than I need her. She said it's also "Okay if she's not happy."

The wording of that sentence was a bit jarring.

I bolted words quickly, "Okay that my mom is not happy? If she's *not* happy!!!" reacting as if it's an emergency, and thinking about the feelings of quickly cleaning the house and the kitchen before she returns home on a school day.

I've somehow learned to hear that rage in places that it doesn't exist.

When my boss tells all of us we are not making enough phone calls, I go out of my way to make 20 phone calls that day-- even if it's 4 pm.

I feel all of this pressure even when my colleague says she will just make the calls on Monday.

I remember when a neighbor came down to my house and yelled at me for something I didn't do. She also wanted to make sure my husband was there to see me get scolded. I guess she thought she'd have more of an audience that way. I have no idea.

I, instead of telling her she was wrong, and she was on her phone at the time, and she didn't even hear what happened, I instead, fell down and almost bowed down at her feet to let her whip me more- -I was eager to please my wrongful abuser. It's what I was taught to do without question.

After that moment, I went on the stairs and cried and cried. And, not long after that, another neighbor who I knew was wrong, and I felt weird about from the very beginning, did the same thing to me, and I let her. And, she was wrong, and I was not wrong. And, anytime I told the story to another person or friend, they were shocked that I had tried to do so much to make it right.

I turned myself upside down and inside out to please beyond human ability.

Disengage

The therapist said to disengage, to cut her off from my life.

The funny thing with boundaries- -my God, if someone tells me that I have to have boundaries one more time- -I've read ALL of the Boundary books already… people don't accept them.

I drew a line in the sand with my dad yesterday, and he did the same thing my mother does. He crossed it trifold. He pushed back. He doesn't listen to me either.

When I graduated with my second masters, it was the same. I wanted to honor his late brother who graduated with a similar degree and dad wondered why I hadn't made the day about honoring himself instead?

All of this time, I felt like an orphan or a child taking care of my own parents, and they were not there for me. Sure, dad paid for my rehearsal dinner. Sure, mom eventually brought the dress. . . but, something was missing.

Texting

Text from mom: "If we were not related, we'd never talk."

Text from mom: "I see that you only answer my texts in emoticons. I get it. Message received."

Text from mom: "I just want you to be really happy. Are you happy? Not just surface happy?"

Text from mom 10 minutes later: "You know I'm always there for you."

Dump cake

Mom made a dump cake, but I couldn't eat it. It was full of nuts and heavy bolts that I, just having dental surgery, couldn't take. I said it was good, but I could only eat soft stuff for a bit.

She got instantly furious and said, "Oh, that's not true!! I had a temporary crown for five years!!"

And, she ran inside and slammed the door.

I'm not honest often. I was sweet, but in the past, I would have just eaten the pie, torn up my mouth, and headed back to the dentist.

Like when my mom gave me (and then took back) one of her six Rolex watches. In a ceremonial way, she gave it to me and said she "wanted me to have something special."

I felt excited that she wanted me to have it. I am not much for fancy things, but it felt like a nice moment.

It took me a week to get it adjusted and then, it was a little snug. I wore it, but not every day. It's just wearing 6k on my wrist made me a little edgy. Of course, no one would believe a teacher that made 40 k a year would have a real Rolex on her sleeve.

But, I wore it as much as I could. But, the problem is, I didn't wear it *when* she was around often enough. If I wasn't *always* wearing the watch, I wasn't always being loyal to her.

Part of me wondered if there was a camera in the watch or some secret notion of power. Perhaps there was because she didn't see me wearing it one too many times and she demanded the watch back.

I brought the watch back. I was a little sad because it seemed like a sweet gesture she was taking back. We had had a moment of sentiment and I hadn't played by her rules so she was taking it away.

She made my sister wear it in front of me. Now, my sister has bigger arms. My sister said it was too tight, and it wouldn't fit.

My mom got angry and angrier. She said, "Wear it Robyn!!!"

My sister said, like the Cinderella stepsister with the shoe that didn't budge, 'It won't fit!'

Mom got red, and started to yell and squished the clasp together. My sister's arm was red, but the watch was on.

Perhaps in her mind it was a point of devotion, a club I hadn't become a devoted member of, I wasn't wearing her charms, hadn't been loyal enough and had betrayed her in disobedience. My sister looked up in an ouch and was just trying to make it through the day.

Guilt technology

I get the guilt calls. If I can't make mom happy, she cries and makes Robyn feel awful. She has Robyn call me, text me, reach out. Robyn, who is now 20, and doesn't know she's being manipulated. It's a triangle, and it hurts.

It hurts to not just do what mom wants. I don't want to hurt her, but I am tired of being hurt over and over again. The relationship has impacted every relationship in my life. And, I am learning it's okay to say no- -even if it's your mom.

Alone at church

I remember I found my spiritual and emotional pacing at church. I know I might have been the only teenager getting up on Sundays and going alone to church, but I was fine with that.

There were the occasional senior or celebratory events when I'd ask mom to come and she came to one. She said it was too long, and when it came to eating together with other people, she felt like time was too expensive.

Grandma used to take me to church. We'd sit on the front pew of Rocky Creek church. My grandma couldn't carry a tune, but we'd sing together on our rides through the countryside. She couldn't figure out how to clap on the right beats, but it didn't matter so much either. She'd rest her feet on the carpet's edge. Her knees were pretty shot. I can still hear the clicking of her cane when she walked two paces behind me.

I found some sort of liking to being in the youth group. So, I kept going. I kept volunteering. I was always there. I felt safe there. I felt comfort. Once we all went out for pizza together. I sat at Pizza Hut on the table, waiting for my food, with five other friends. About twenty or so others filled the room. It was my perfect idea of a feast. Music was there. Drinks on the table. Mom came in to see me. She was clearly angry about something.

And, with the same attitude she had about me "quitting that Baptist crap," she grabbed my hand, and dragged me out of the Pizza Hut. I left my friends, the pizza and that warm comfortable feeling. I didn't know know. I just know I had to leave, and now.

Being an adult in a child's world

Now, I never knew what would cause her mood changes. Once she got into drinking a bit and drove us clear into the apartment access gate. It damaged the car a little. And, she woke up from that moment and cried and apologized with such sincerity that I hardly remembered it had happened.

I'd watch her go in and out of relationships. I'd see her with herself and sometimes she'd compete with me though I didn't notice it until years later. She'd flirt with my boyfriends.

Looking back, she and I were staying with a guy named Robert. I was sitting on the floor in I guess "my room" playing a record, and she came in to talk to me. It was a nice affectionate time. And, then she said she "had to go back to Robert's room." I don't remember being afraid or worried, just lonely.

Once, I guess they wanted to sleep late, Robert suggested that I could just walk across the street to the other apartments. He said, just across the median, I could squeeze through the gate poles and play in that playground.

Looking back, I wondered how he knew I'd fit through those poles, how I'd be safe to play alone and how I'd cross the street. I must have been about seven years old. I remember wondering if I'd get caught, if I'd get in trouble. But, most of all, I felt alone.

No one else was on that playground with me. The gear was cold. It was early. If I played with anyone, I played with ghosts.

Remarried

About two years later, mom remarried. He was a nice guy. We got close just about the time she was ready to leave him. Two years into marriage or so, it was over.

My brother was born, and mom says that I "practically raised him." With her as a single mom, we always had to work together. I watched him while she went away to exercise classes. I pushed the stroller. And, wherever I went, whether it be out with friends, anything, she'd ask me 'What about your brother?' He was with me everywhere.

Some days I wonder why our relationship is not better than it is. I mean, we hardly talk, he's cold. And, I can't fix it.

The best way I have determined to fix it is not to care when he doesn't call, reach back or love me in the way I need to be loved with simple conversations. I keep waiting around for him to want to know his nephews, to want to hear about me and to be around.

It was the hardest thing in the world to leave my mom's house at 22. He was in the driveway when I left.

My first apartment. My first big job. He was standing there, and I missed him so much. I blamed myself for years that I couldn't continue to carry him, and be there for him as he grew. My mom made sure that I knew how 'he cried on the driveway' as I drove away. I asked him later what happened. He said nothing of that sort.

Sitter

At that time, I was 23 and engaged. I had lived away from home for about a year, and I thought about coming back. I thought it would be great to save for my wedding. I thought it would be good. Mom was about to have another baby too at the age of 42, and I think she wanted help. In fact, I know she wanted help with that.

But, then, as I told her about coming home, she didn't respect that I wanted to save up for a wedding. She didn't seem easy or sentimental about having me home. And, when my sister was born, I was sad I couldn't be there, but grateful for the reality that hit. I told mom that no I didn't 'want to be her sitter' even if I 'was the only person she trusted.' I wanted to be her 'sister.'

Mom disowned me again. She said I was 'not her daughter.'

Leaps of faith

When the tables were flipped, and I needed her to watch my baby, she wasn't available. My son was about three months old or so and my friend, who just had a baby prematurely, and it was a sad hard story. She and I had been through so much together, and I had to travel across town to be there. And, I wasn't about to bring my healthy baby to my friend's baby shower. Her baby was still in the NICU.

I got to mom's house, stressed. With nursing, you have to pump and prepare for almost a week in advance. I packed everything. I had it all ready. I wasn't quite ready to leave him for the first time. But, this was Lana and she needed me. I wanted to be there for her. I needed to be there for her. I had planned to leave my son for almost an hour. I had just enough time to get to the shower, stay for a bit and get back to feed my son, if needed.

When I arrive at mom's house, she's not there. I call and call. And, I hear her on the phone. She has had a little to drink and has forgotten about me coming by. She forgot that I was driving an hour to her house that day. I thought that was rare since we didn't see each other that much. I could tell she wasn't in her best place. She said she'd be home in about 20 minutes or so.

So I stayed at the house and paced and wondered and worried.

She arrived sober, fine and seemed okay. I didn't want to leave, but I felt like my son would be fine. My stepdad was there. And, my friend needed me. I left, and then hurried back to see my mom trying to feed my baby. It wasn't going well. He wouldn't take the food. She was very stressed. And, he was very unhappy. I tossed the bottle, fed the kid, thanked her just enough to inflate her spirit and went home exhausted.

She watched my children again about 10 years later- -all three boys. She tried to bathe my youngest kid with sensory issues because every kid "MUST have a bath" every day, and she was so emotionally damaged by the experience I thought she'd never or maybe she hasn't still, recovered. I try to tell her things, but she doesn't listen. Baths, at that time, made him feel scared. I had to do things a certain way. With him, it can't be, as she raised me- -my way or the highway.

When I came home from the only second evening I've had alone in 10 years, I had to nurse my mom back to life. She was the victim, and I was her debtor.

She didn't bother to call me at the moment all of this was happening. She didn't reach out and ask for help. She didn't think she didn't know it all. And my son didn't give up. He had hit his head on the bathtub when he struggled so much. And mom, when I got there, was emotionally cowering in a corner.

It doesn't work

I'd like her to have a better relationship with my children, but it doesn't work like that. I feel like I have to fight for them.

When my kid wouldn't eat the French fry when she wanted him to, she was all over the place. She said, 'When he's in jail…'

I said, 'Mom, I'll deal with Aspergers….

Son, you eat the fry when you want, just one and then you can go play.'

He thought for 20 seconds, ate the fry, and then went to go play.

Centimeters at a time

I don't have to be right here. But, I am learning I have to fight for my rights- -if not for me- - but, this go around, for my children.

It's getting easier if only in centimeters at a time.

I know she loves me. I know she's always loved me in her own way. But, it's like she can't love past losing me- -losing me to her will.

And, I can't help that. I can't help her. I suppose the hardest part of trying to break away- -of trying to not grieve space is when I look up in the mirror, and I see her looking back. Or, I see my father too in my brooding motions. I see her in how I fold the towels. I see her when I lose my temper. I see her when I take on too much.

Lightning

My friend wrote this song about static. Every time I hear it, I cry. I heard it live last night, and I cried again. And, I think about the song almost every day. I think about the stuff that sticks to me.

I try to trust mom. I try to let her in over and over. I ask for help.

And, she said she'd be there for me. I was working again away from home full time and in grad school full time. I asked if she'd watch the kids so I could study. She said she'd love to. So, I drove 30 minutes to her house to study. And the kids were running around acting like kids. I had my laptop open in the kitchen. I began to read and take notes.

She walked in wet from a shower and glared at me. She asked me "Why are you not watching the kids?" I packed up my stuff and left. I said it was a nice visit, but I needed to go home to study.

She didn't get it

She didn't get it often. I took Algebra I four times. I took it in the 7th grade too early. I took it in the 8th grade to get it again. Then, I took it and finally got it in the ninth grade. When I had to take it again in college, I spent so much time in the tutorial room. My professor coincidentally retired the following year.

She didn't get how hard I had to work to get the grade. I have a picture of me sitting on the kitchen floor going over a math assignment again, and she's calling on me to go vacuum something right now. Nothing could wait.

I finally found some peace when the Aggie neighbor next door would tutor me. He was an engineer and he could explain math very well to me. He was fun too. It was peaceful. He had an old scrawny dog named Garry and a scratched up couch.

From Private to Public

In school studies, I was lopsided. I attended a private school from first to sixth grade. The teachers were pretty good, but not always in the academics of teaching math or science. I remember Mr. Bigalow. He was about 180. We didn't have a science lab to learn in. We had desks and papers and tests. But, he did introduce me to the story of the Titanic which fascinated me.

The majority of the teachers taught Bible, spelling, reading and English studies very well. And, although I found out later, I was about two years ahead in mathematics in public school, I was behind in a variety of other ways.

I had been sheltered from the world. I had only known the same 14 students during those six years. An entire lunchroom of students, for the entire school, was about 200 students. I could walk into lunch and sit with the entire third grade.

It was just us. We were brothers and sisters. We watched each other grow. We watched each other fail. We cheered each other on. We listened to each other cry in the bathrooms. We took gymnastics together. We were all part of the basketball team. We were all part of the drill team. We were cheerleaders. We were all the same.

Many of us still talk thirty years later. Lyn is a missionary in England with a family of boys. Ellen is an accountant with two girls in Paris. Mindy is a teacher in Houston. Michell is a busy mom. Nancy is a Hollywood director. Kaye died our senior year.

I remember mid-way sixth grade year, my mom told me that my grandmother was too close.

She said, "She's taking you away from me."

She had moved to our hometown to help out, and mom was feeling like I was seeing too much of her.

And, coincidentally, grandma was also paying for my private school education. So, mid-year sixth grade, mom took me out of my private school home.

Ms. Phillips heard and grabbed me tight and cried and cried. I didn't know why she was so sad. I didn't know why she didn't want me to leave. I was nearly failing her English class at the time. And, she had scolded me a zillion times for chewing gum and talking too much. It took her a long time to physically let go of me.

The big view

Walking into that junior high, everything changed. I had my "tour" from the office aide.

She said, "You have like 15 minutes left of class. . .that's a LONG time. . .you might want to hang out a bit."

I declined and walked into the restless and very noisy math class. The class was learning something I learned in the fourth grade. We were asked to add and subtract fractions. I went up to the board, solved the problem in a fraction of the time of the other students. I sat down. The room was a zoo.

I don't remember the teacher. I never looked up.

I stepped into English class, and it was a zoo too. The teacher gave us all one paragraph to practice reading, and we were going to go through the story with our paragraphs reading out loud. I was given my paragraph and I said something I shouldn't have. And, it's not that it was what I believed, but I was repeating what my mom had said over and over.

I told the black student in front of me that he was slow "because he was black." and I have no idea why I said that. It was a terrible thing to say. I was so numb and just in fight or flight mode that I was just repeating mom's ad-libs from home. The whole room got quiet and stood in ready-to-punch me mode. The teacher quieted us down and she sent us outside to "settle things."

I stood outside alone with the student who chewed me out. And, I took it. I let the student verbally abuse me. It came naturally to be beat up that way and maybe I was soothed by it. But, after that beating, we walked in. The student had his hands up like a champion. I had my head down when we walked in. The students cheered and I went into my seat like a dog with his tail down. The class moved forward with us reading our paragraphs.

I am not sure how prejudiced mom is. I just remember the moments when I feared for my life when she acted in a prejudicial way.

We were living in an apartment complex with a few rugged edges- -meaning I tried not to walk alone in the rougher side of the city. Mom and I were at the pool. I don't know what happened to make her suddenly so angry. But, she yelled, "I hate Nigg@#$!" She was raging!

I looked around us fearing for our lives. I knew at any moment, she could be shot. I looked at the people around us. I looked up, and pleaded as the nine-year-old child. I remember fearing for my mother's life because she had no filter and she'd say things at exactly the wrong times. She was all rage sometimes without thinking about the consequences.

Looking for the good

It's not that all of the memories are bad. I know she cares. It's just that it's not like she can handle normal needs. I remember my junior year of high school, and I was invited to the awards ceremony. We waited. I got one award, and she *really* wanted to go. We ended up leaving just before I got the "Journalism Writer of Year" award. My teacher was so sad that I missed the surprise opportunity. But, mom, just couldn't wait. She couldn't sit still. And, as the energy was rising, I couldn't handle her fire either. We left, and she felt better. Then, I felt better.

Parenting

When she lost the baby at 40, I did my best to take care of her. She had just told me she was expecting with her long-time boyfriend. She looked me in the eyes with a slight smile, and told me. I was happy for her, but feeling a bit twisted. Two weeks later, she miscarried. The guy went distant. She said she was in the elevator at the doctor's office when she lost her mind. The news that there was no longer a heartbeat nearly killed her.

And, the doctor gave her medicine, and she cried in her bed for days. I didn't have a car at the time, so I walked a mile-rather-ran a mile to get to the pharmacy to get her medication. She was whirling in tears and crying nonstop. I picked up her prescription somehow and walked out into the parking lot. I saw my Sunday school teacher. I asked for a ride.

I said, "I walked here to help my mom. She's sick. She lost the baby. Can you take me home? It's kind of a ways away. I need to get her these meds."

She asked, "How did you get here?"

I said, "I ran."

She said, "I didn't even know your mom was married. Wow. Yeah. Sure get in."

She drove me home. I remember it was comforting to have a ride back, having someone to take care of me for a bit. The teacher asked more questions. I answered matter of factly and just moved forward.

My mom got her meds. She looked up, and didn't seem to notice I had gone, she continued crying. I shut the door to her dark room and went on to study.

A few days later, we celebrated my birthday. We had a very quiet meal. No one talked. The baby, "Andy" had died on my birthday. We forcibly talked through the meal and had polite chatter. It was a dark evening for celebration.

Pretty pictures

This morning I saw a pretty picture of a young woman. She had obviously spent money on herself, time to do her hair and makeup and she was feeling beautiful too. And, I felt frustrated and jealous and angry.

I didn't feel like it was my turn to be pretty. I had this nagging feeling like I had to wait, I was being punished and it was time to lay low and be invisible. And, I don't know where I got this feeling. I don't often buy myself clothes (unless I donate a bunch and "earn it" somehow). I don't often buy myself makeup or do my nails.

I don't feel obliged to do those things for myself. I go to the dentist, yearly physicals, etc., but beauty, I don't always feel like it's my turn. It's like, inside, I feel like if mom is not happy with me, as I am afraid she's not happy with me right now, that I don't get to shine, that I am not allowed to be happy, free or to have a good time or to feel good. I feel like the dog who has been put in the corner and shamed. I am afraid that sometimes I put myself there because it's something I am used to. I also feel like it's something I just don't deserve.

Yesterday, I bought myself two dresses and a shirt from a discount online place. They just looked lovely. I had originally seen two more items, but I looked at my budget and cut it down. I tried to be as practical as possible. I picked an off-of-the-shoulder dress and theorized on how often I could wear it, a pretty shirt that was more for date nights and concerts and a long dress that I could wear to church. I don't have shoes yet for the long dress, but I thought I'd worry about that later.

It felt wonderful to clear away closets and clean out drawers and sift away the drama. I donated clothes that might have been almost new because they didn't make me feel okay. I put away things that I had worn a couple of times that had gotten short, or changed in laundry adventures. I donated a pair of pants that reminded me of a former boss that brought me down. I lined up the closet with just clothes I feel awesome in.

I lined up three new pairs of pants from Beall's that fit perfectly. I even washed them before I hung them up. I feel great in them. It was like I was taking care of myself. I felt good. It's interesting how small gestures like these can be therapeutic.

Overalls

Once my mom got into an overall phase. My sister was about a year old. I was in my twenties. My mom was in her early forties. She point-blank asked me if I liked her overalls. I said she was too old to wear overalls. She was fuming. Looking back, I had associated overalls with children and she had, in fact, too associated with youth. She didn't talk to me for a while.

Married to other people

When my mom was married to her current husband, she had my fiance' marry them. He had just been licensed as a Baptist minister, so he was able to marry people. He also, 13 years later, married my dad to my stepmom. So, I can say he married my mom and dad to separate people.

The day of my mom's wedding, I was about five minutes late. She was in the kitchen. She was flustered. She was angry. She was anxious. I was late because I was bringing her flowers. She didn't want the flowers.

She was angry and didn't understand my need to make the moment special.

Within five minutes or so my step-dad mosied into the kitchen with his arm in a cloth cast, no shirt and only purple running shorts. He put his arm on the bar. My mom stood behind the kitchen counter.

And he said, "Let's do this."

My fiance', who had driven five hours from working with church youth at summer camp to be there, was wearing a suit and using the glass kitchen table as his pulpit.

Within about ten minutes they were married. My step-dad moved back into the other room to watch TV, and mom finished the dishes. My half-sister was around there somewhere toddling through the house.

Trying to be the adult this time

Once mom invited us to go to Alabama. We went thinking it would be easy. It wasn't so bad. It just took planning. Three small children on a plane is tough. We were determined to make it work.

My mom had ornaments all over the place. She had this music box town that lit up on the table. My youngest son, who has emotional issues, and is on the autism spectrum wanted to touch it.

He wasn't talking yet at the time. In fact, he whispered but mainly to his brothers, and definitely not when my mom is in the room. It's the second day we were tired. Mom goes crazy.

She screamed, "Spank his hands!! Or Beat the hell out of him when he does that!"

I feel like she's beating me up when she said that.

At that moment, I was a child again. So, I spanked my son's hands, and told him not to touch. He cried and she approved. I was punished, and she approved. She was happy because it was her house, and she was in charge.

Looking back, I wished I could have fought back, and said "Let's just move the house." Or, better, yet, "Let him explore it safely." But, at the time, none of those options appeared possible.

The next night, her professor friends came by, and they talked for hours and hours. I hardly felt like I was in the room. She was so impressed by them. One was a lawyer, one was 26 dating the 55-year-old-something lawyer. And, they were the center of attention. Growing tired, I went to bed when they began drinking and playing with guns.

The next day, I don't know how this happened, maybe it was the cat, but a plastic cup of Cheerios fell on the floor. I didn't see it. I was putting a child down to nap. About 10-15 Cheerios fell on the floor. And, I listened from the room downstairs, and hear mom frantically vacuuming the kitchen for about 25 minutes. She was banging things around and making a big ruckus.

Later that day, I realized she isn't talking to me. I didn't get it. About a day later, 18 hours later, it was time to pack up the car and leave. We had traveled nine hours on a plane with three children, and it was time to go. I said goodbye to everyone lined up by the door. I know I cleaned up the room we stayed in. Packing for five isn't easy.

Mom looked at me staring me into the eyes.

She said, "Cheerios. You made a mess and didn't clean it up."

I said, "I honestly don't know *what* you're talking about."

She glared, "*You* spilled the Cheerios!"

And, that was the end of that moment. I left without a goodbye.

Zoo

That reminds me of the time she came to visit, but I wasn't sure about going to the zoo. My son had a touch of a cold, and frankly, I was tired. So I told her we'd probably not be going to the zoo.

Then, about two hours later, I thought we could go. And, so I called her. She said she was already going with her doctor friends and their twins. I told her we were coming. And, I said, we'd be there in thirty minutes or so. I knew she was going back to Alabama the next day, and I thought the quality time would be good.

I got to the zoo. And, I called her.

She says "What?"

And the phone is sounding fuzzy and I can feel that she's angry.

I said clearly and slowly. "We are here. We are at the zoo. Come see us. We can join you. I gave my son some cold meds, and we are making it work."

She hung up the phone. And, I thought she must be within three minutes of me. And, her three grandchildren were right here too. And, I look around and see she's not around.

I think surely she's searching for us too. I give it a minute, and then decide to walk through the zoo alone.

About two hours later, I headed to the car. Before I got to the car, I tried again to reach her. I told her we were still there, and wanted to say goodbye and be careful on the trip back home.

She held her ground. Like when we all went to the zoo together with my friend Susan, and I put Susan's ideas first, mom was so annoyed, she said, "We have to do what *Susie* wants!!" Mom was so upset with me. I was just trying to make it work by putting my friend first. I have a tendency to over-give in all directions. And, sometimes I get lost in the process.

I heard mom in situations like these. Like when a lady at the zoo gives me a look of disapproval because my son walked too fast over her foot. I stopped and spanked my son and let her know I am disciplining my child to please the woman. The woman was appalled. And, later I was appalled too. I had just seen my mom, and felt the need to punish so that I'd temporarily please her. Mom is everywhere. All of the time.

The kid was just being a kid. In crowds, kids make mistakes. In every day's settings, kids make mistakes. People make mistakes. Cats. Kids. Invisible men spill Cheerios. And, it's okay if it happens.

Yesterday

Yesterday, I drove an hour to see old friends. I got five minutes into the drive, and heard one friend won't make it. She's tired. It's hard because I am meeting her in the park a block from her house. But, it's an Easter egg hunt, and I assume there's a reason why. I assume this means other people will be there for me to talk to.

The kids played with friends like no time had passed. A sitter that watched them was happy to see them. She met a great guy. Her son was off to college. We were both so different we barely recognized each other.

The boys and I took a walk along the just now grass riverbed path. We saw rock snowmen all over the place. And art made smiles on the ground. The place had a certain kind of cheer. The boys ran and ran in the circle. I didn't worry as much as I once did. I used to worry about snakes and cars, but not so much about them in this place.

We played with bamboo doorways and caterpillars marching across the gravel path.

As I was leaving, I felt the tug. I went to see my other "family."

My son's former music teacher, Leo. We knock on his door. Me and the three boys have a blast. We talked for nearly an hour. We laughed and played music together.

He heard I've got a writing gig with a major musician. He encouraged me.

Leo says, "Anytime you write good press, it's a good thing. Musicians love that! Helping with *that* guy? That's *the* big time. Getting pictures too? That's big time!"

He cared about what I had to say. He shared his stories. And, I listened to every single word.

He laughed and said, "I'm not making fun of anyone, but we are the young people at the bowling alley. Older players do this."

He hobbles in centimeters with his legs and motions laying down the ball. "It takes very little skill, but wouldn't you know, they get a strike almost every time?" He laughed.

He brought out his bowling ball and fancy bag. The size 14 ball is too heavy to hold. My oldest son tried to pick it up.

Leo says, "Don't drop it on my foot." He talked about his bowling shoes too. He celebrates his matching shirt.

We laugh, and he walks me to the driveway. He doesn't want me to leave. It makes me happy. I took the moment to stop and take the risk to see him. I am glad I rang the doorbell twice. Glad my sons insisted on seeing him too.

I smile for days knowing it made my heart whole to see him and to know he missed me too. And, it reminded me to remember not to rely on email for those talks. He's not awesome at email.

I love that some relationships work. It's the best feeling to feel appreciated and loved right back when you need it.

What is real?

These days I have trouble trusting if a relationship is real. I have trouble understanding what is stable and won't leave. With mom, things would come and go all of the time.

Through counseling, I know her love for me is there, but the emotional tug of war left me stranded with my head filled with slamming doors and phones. If she didn't agree, that's all it would be.

And, I am surprised at when things aren't the same way in other places. I also have a tendency to feel like the world is coming down on me. I feel like if my boss is upset with me, I've for sure, lost my job. I take punishment with allegiance.

I also take words of encouragement with holy delight. If I can work like a dog to write a story that makes someone smile, I feel like I am the richest person in the world. If I have given something of joy in my words, my whole world feels full. My life feels complete.

I heard once we crave what we need the most. When I hear kind words, I either devour them or ignore them to stay humble. I read this week that if I am doubting something I am doing (creative), then I am doing something right. It is the strangest thing. I also was reminded to listen to that voice inside that says change this. Clip this story. Take out the gooey heart and just leave what you see- -the story you feel will still be there. My Hollywood friend from grade school taught me that.

And, the story with less, is always better.

I remember the positive moments

I remember when she paid for my reconstructive surgery, but when I wanted to celebrate afterwards, she wasn't around.

When I finally conceived my first child, we went maternity shopping. She doted on me, bought me a "Due in June" shirt, and it was a big moment. She was more excited than I was. Then, when I told her I was expecting the second, she asked well what about the first? And the same happened with the third two years later- -except that time she didn't talk to me for a while.

Finding *my* happy

And, I don't know what to do with my happiness. I have finally found happiness. It doesn't depend on the job I don't have. I am writing on my own terms. I am making happiness by reaching out and taking chances. At times, it's terrifying. Every day there is less "Static on my wings" (Dawn and Hawkes).

Last night, I was able to see my new favorite musician. And, the thing is, I don't know if he understood what I was saying. I pray he did. I told him how rare he was- -how rare people like us are- -feelers and perceivers. And, I told him he's in my house framed next to Willie and my grandpa. And, I told him I thought he was brave for how he lays it all on stage. I said it takes guts. He said he appreciated that, and gave me a hug.

Later, I sent him the positive review I wrote. He liked it. Now, my third favorite artist has read my work. It was the happiest time.

Childhood glass

I remember when mom got mad at dad. They were only together until I was about four or five, but when they were together, things were up and down a lot. Once she got mad at my dad and threw a Sunkist bottle at him. Back in the early 80s, the soda cans were glass.

She all-out threw the glass at his face. She must have been really angry at him. The glass cut his face kind of like how the dog grabbed my face about a year before that when my dad "wasn't watching me."

He was bleeding. I don't know why they were fighting. It's like things were always building up to the volcanic moment of explosion.

And, then, things exploded. But, then, within a few moments, she grabbed a towel and was "sorry."

We left quickly to go to urgent care. We waited a long time, and I think he got stitches. It was weird and scary because she was so angry. And, then, all of a sudden, she was sorry.

It's like she was in this pattern of anger and then punishing herself for her own actions. She was in a cycle of anger, and then sorry and then guilt and then trying to earn love again. Then, she'd earn it and manipulate it. Then, that person would be unable to talk about their feelings and drift away. Then, she'd get angry at them, punish them, sometimes they'd come back, sometimes they wouldn't.

Good friends were good friends for a very short time. She'd love them too closely. Friends would become family very quickly and then, they'd say something wrong and lose her love almost immediately. They'd say something like they were voting for Hillary, for example, and she'd never talk to them again.

Things were always skewed into the boxes of the stories she said they were. Things were never allowed to breathe or to be explained. It was slamming phones and agreeing to her feelings that helped. And, of course, groveling to become lower than her shoes, to eventually, hopefully, earn her love back. When you had her love, you felt like you had everything. You had all of the allies on your side. But, when the tide turned, it was duck and cover.

I am just now learning how to "be selfish" and to argue back. I am learning how to say no, and that I have rights. I am learning that I am not worthless when I do something wrong. I am not lower than the lowest part. I do not have to bow down like a dog licking his wounds.

Healing space

Lately, since I've had some space from my mom, I've felt so strong and powerful and great, not great like great, but well, great and big. It's scary to feel this way. And, I'm afraid I've made some mistakes with this new power along the way. I don't let people put me in a box anymore.

So, I've pulled a Leo. My musician teacher friend- -he taught me this. And, I've decided to dust it off my shoulders.

I am dusting off those stories not published, and writing my own and well, still taking pictures and still showing off what I can do and still not giving up and getting 500 hits a week on my blog. He taught me to just keep going. Move onto the next project. Don't think so much about what didn't work. Concentrate on what is working. And, move!

I also learned how to take more deep breaths, not to take things personally and remember that most of the time it's not about me, it's the other person's issues.

Despite how great I feel, all of that- -putting myself out there, writing two amazing well-recognized stories in two weeks- -giving my all for nothing-makes me feel like hiding out for a week at least.

I am so close, but I don't know what I am so close to, and that scares me a bit, makes me retreat, makes me feel like I'm going to blow it all, makes me hide, makes me hurt, makes me feel like my whole life I've been waiting not to be put in a corner, and now that I'm out there in the ring, I don't know what to do with the power.

Working again away from home

I finally feel happy these days. I have things I am sorting out, but I feel happy. My marriage is working again for the first time in seven years. I have settled down to the fact that I don't like my job, and it may be awhile before I have the job I want. And, I am using my time to write.

I am using my time to refocus my journey and to take better care of myself and my family. I have time to do those important things for them without guilt. I have time to toss in two loads of laundry. I have time to take a lap around the block. I have time to catch up on my Grey's Anatomy, time to take the photography class and take the homework shot eight times to get it right. It might feel like too much time sometimes. But, I am learning how to deal with that too.

As I am finding my work pace, mom texts me. She says, "I just want you to be happy."

I let it go because I am working, and I don't have time for mind games. Looking back I see she might just be reaching out because she needs to be needed, but I realize I also need to *not need* her too. And, I need her to not need me so much as well.

An hour later, as she is waiting by the phone; she texts again about some arbitrary thing. I texted back a rainbow picture just to check in.

I am busy. And I don't have time. Heck, I've been yelled at by bosses because she called at work and took too much of my time. Sometimes, I just have to focus on the task in front of me.

Then, she texted, "I see only smiles and three letter words. I get the message. Message received."

She created the war in her head. She created the drama that wasn't there. If she really wanted to make it not about her somehow, she would have just texted me to say hello and to check on me or she'd call and ask how everyone was.

So, it made me angry because I was finally centered. I finally had let her go, and well, just like the therapist said to do, and she, like the other therapist said, "needed me more than I needed her."

The therapist saw my dramatic change in disposition when I mentioned my mom. He said, "She's no good for you. She's not okay. Disconnect."

I said, "What about her?"

He said, "What about her?"

Perspectives

So, I left the therapist room and disconnected with my mom and disconnected with the guilt. And, it felt great, until her text yesterday. It's just not good. She's a mess, and I need her to stop waiting around for me. I need her to stop doing harm and telling me things that are not true. She told me I was the one who caused my youngest to be autistic and emotionally disturbed.

I spoke up about that in a counseling meeting with a pastor in the room. The pastor, who doesn't even know me, said "whoever told you that is evil."

I remember three years into having children. My OBGYN, who had been with me through a series of trials and really painful circumstances, was frustrated with me. Now, he was the kind of of guy, married and with three children, but as Cee described him, 'He's so nice you'd think he was gay.'

He was honestly one of the nicest people I've ever met. He was the first OB to ask me how I was doing emotionally with a finally-successful pregnancy.

I walked into the OBs office that day. I am sure I was grumpy in the exam room. I don't know what my deal was that day. Some days I get deflated. It's like there's this invisible model always putting me in my place, the moment I get happy. It's this ghost telling me to deflate.

My OB leaves the room in a huff. He says, "When are you going to open your eyes, and realize that you are a pretty and intelligent woman?"

Finding that power

And, now that I am finding some success in my writing and joy in serving others by doing what I love, I am feeling inflated. I am feeling that power.

I am realizing my OB was right. I have been trained to look at all of my flaws and not look at the good things about me.

My mom comes to my house and points out every dish left in the sink.

And, it's hard because yes, I worry "what about her?" I worry that the world will feel flat when she passes (*Anywhere But Here* movie), but also, I feel like I have the right to be happy, at last.

Peeing on a log

It seemed my parents are the same- -always putting me in my place- -less than them. I remember the first most humiliating experience for me. I was about five and we were camping. My father took a picture of me peeing on a log. He saved it and laughed and printed it out. He showed others and thought it was the "cutest" funniest thing ever.

It was the most embarrassing thing for me. He was my dad. He was supposed to protect me. He wasn't allowed to make me feel small. But, he did.

I remember when I was about five years old finding some kind of pill on the kitchen counter. It was the kind in a capsule you can break in half. I broke it in half while he was busy to see all of the beads break out. He got so mad at me. I ran out of the room. I didn't know why he was so angry. I was just curious and the pill was sitting right there in the middle of the off-white countertop. It looked like an old get-skinny pill, but I didn't think he needed to lose weight at the time. He was a skinny guy at the time. His anger scared me. He, like my mom, would yell and have big tantrums. He'd grit his teeth and throw his voice like a lion.

My most happy memory of him and I was when he was living in north Arkansas, and he surprised me by buying a pink and grey ten-speed bike. We used it to bike all over the place.

But, then, times changed and things got busy. He did help me with state school projects. And, he tried to teach me fractions, but he got angry. And, ever since then, I still have this mental block about fractions. I just cave and think about being yelled at for not getting it. I melt like that nine-year-old child.

We did enjoy the state projects together. He did help, but there was a time or two when alcohol took over.

During my jr high year, I had a project that was due on Monday, and I waited for him to help me, but we were visiting one of his girlfriends.

He got so drunk. He was puking out of the passenger car window and mumbling all sorts of words. We got to her place and heroically, she took me to get the project board at some craft store, and I put the whole project together in one day and without dad's help.

He didn't always know how to be a dad. I was embarrassed to have gotten to the state capitol with the other kids, and in the bathroom, I was scolded. I was a mess. I was only 13, and I still needed help to pack. But, I didn't have that kind of help. I hadn't even packed a hair brush, In fact, I think there was an orange juice stain on my shirt.

I walked into the bathroom and a girl my age was combing her hair. I was in the top 6 state spot, but my hair was a mess. I had come kind-of alone. My dad was staying in another hotel as there wasn't a place for parents. I was staying with another friend who was a contestant, but we were not traveling in the same competition circle that day. We were two 13-year-old girls pretty much living alone for that day. I looked at my hair in that bathroom, and I asked the stranger girl if I could borrow her brush. She said, "sure" and she smiled at me. I needed that smile so much. The world felt so cold that moment.

The girl's mom stepped out of the stall and took one look at lost me, and looked down on me. She said, "*We* don't do THAT." And she ushered her child out of the bathroom as if we had never talked.

I left the bathroom and my dad took me to the gift shop to get a hairbrush. I was mortified.

Girlfriends

Dad had lots of girlfriends. There was a curly-haired one. The red head. The blonde he married. The curly haired one is one we spent lots of time with. She saved the project day for me when dad was puking. She also taught me how to use a tampon.

She was visiting dad once while he was dating the second blonde he married later. They were eating dinner together. It was me as the third wheel. And, it was about 11 pm. I had lost my voice. I was about 14. My dad told me to go to the pay phone to see if my former boyfriend, who lived next door to my uncle's house, wanted to hang out tonight.

I called and looking back, it was very weird because my ex-boyfriend's mom answered and she heard my voice was cracking. She must have assumed I was crying. I just had laryngitis. She said it was too late to hang out. I said okay.

When we got in the car after dinner, dad said that his girlfriend had wanted him to stay overnight, but it didn't work out. I looked back later and realized he wanted me to find a place to go, and when that didn't work out, his plans couldn't be changed. And, I even then said, "What about Rachel?"

I couldn't believe I had the nerve to ask that looking back. Rachel was the girl he was living with at the time, whom he later had two children with and stayed with for about 24 years. He didn't make a comment back. We went back to Rachel's house and the night was over.

Awkward birthday candles

I remember, for my 16th or 17th birthday, my mom told my new boyfriend at the time to get some friends together for a surprise party. At the time, we had just moved to my third high school and I had no friends. So, my boyfriend invited four of his friends. My friend Elizabeth was there from an hour away, and that was a nice surprise. We all sat around the kitchen table awkwardly while I blew out my candles. We also ate pizza.

With mom hovering about the kitchen table, it was like an appointment for a staged Thanksgiving meal. The highlight was when she looked at everyone, and said, "If you ever want to know what a girl you're dating will look like when she's older, look at her mom!"

With mom's boob job, and my breasts that didn't come in, I'd do all I could to dress myself up, but nothing could compete with her sports bra attire and confidence.

Enmeshed

Over time, I learned about this word--enmeshment.

Enmeshment in relationships is not healthy. You never own another person. And, if someone else steps in a new direction, has a success you haven't had before, if you feel lonely, that's not them betraying you. That's not them being selfish for not waiting on you. That's not abandonment. It's natural for friendships to move apart and then sometimes come closer together. Relationships are always in motion.

Sometimes things only last for a season. In fact, the greatest way you can love someone is to let them go- -let them be true to themselves and to grow in the way they need to grow. True friendship is loving someone for free and not expecting anything back. I've learned it's okay to need people, but inside, I've also learned it's hard for me to believe they won't leave me.

I wish I could say, "So mom, I didn't text you back right away.

I was in the middle of something. Or, maybe I just didn't want to text. Maybe, I just wanted space.

Maybe I just wanted it to be okay to want space. Did you ever consider how your actions impact me?"

Funny clouds

I can count the days when drugs were involved and funny pipes and smells impacted the room. And, I wondered why everyone was circled up around this smokey flower basket in the middle of the room. And why did everyone think everything was funny? And, why was that man without his shirt and rubbing his nipples in a circular motion? Why was everyone so happy? And, why am I watching all of this like a party I am not invited to? These people seem so tall to me, but in this state, they look like children. And, I was just a child at the time. Just a child.

But, I am not a child now. And, I don't want to be put into that box anymore. I don't want to be treated that way anymore. I don't want to be mistreated, or manipulated.

It's hard to be hard though. If she's unhappy with me, I feel it from a million miles away. I feel her brooding over me and mad at me. I feel if she's feeling violent. I can still feel her storm. If she's not happy, I was not allowed to be happy. The first therapist said that it was okay if my mom wasn't happy. And, I try to repeat that to myself when it's too much.

Some days it's too much

So, I wonder when it will end. I wonder when the war will be over. I keep thinking if she had more to do. I keep thinking if she felt more power. I keep thinking if she had a career of her own.

I know the answer is the same. I know that I am allowed to be happy at any time.

And, she says I am wrong. Like, when I know she said she has loaded guns (I don't know if they have safety on them) in her bedroom drawers. I asked her to put the guns away when my children are around.

She said, "Yeah, sure. I'll do that" with a laugh and a scoff.

She said, "The kids don't even go into that wing of the house."

I know the house is 10k square feet. I know they don't go onto *that* side, but I can't be okay with that.

She said her daughter, at 17, even has a gun in her room, and she's been trained to use it.

I've got a kid with special needs, and I got a really smart one that likes to take things apart just for fun.

Even with the kids, I'm still fighting my way through this. I say what I need, and I get pushed down.

Car shaming

I remember we were at a hotel she was staying at and mom was so embarrassed by me in front of the valet. That seems to be a trend. Mom needs to look cool in front of strangers and people like the valet who are just people that are strangers and really don't care.

My car looked like a car when three kids lived there. It was a mess. But, as a full-time working mom in grad school with three children, it had to be. Well, honestly, it's usually like that. I try to care about twice a year.

But she told the valet, I was a mess. I leaned out to make her happy as I've been taught to bend to her every whim.

I told the valet, "Just like she said, I'm a pig."

I was hoping it would appease my mom just like when I broke up with the guy I was dating for four months in high school. Just kept sending her vials of blood to make her happy. And, it's never enough.

I wonder when she's going to be there for me. When it won't always be about her.

I keep wondering when she will want to be with her grandchildren for them and not scold them for not fitting her mold.

Last time my oldest was with her, she bought him shoes and he couldn't make up his mind. So she told him with a laugh, "I'll beat the hell out of you if you don't make up your mind."

My son made a decision. By the end of that one day stay, he had his head down for the next three days following. He told me he didn't want to return. I told mom in a nice way my son didn't like being told she would beat the hell out of him. He didn't think it was funny. She smiled, and rolled her eyes and accused us of being too sensitive.

It's not my job

Perhaps, the strongest thing I have found in counseling and in completing my masters in counseling is that she is in charge of her own happiness. I need to be my own best friend and I need self-care.

I have learned to be a lot more selfish.

I read today that Borderline Personality Disorder parents give a series of tests. When I don't answer, she feels abandoned, even if I was asleep or not able to talk. And, I feel I will never be able to give her what she wants. Any less than what she wants is never enough.

I talked to Ellen yesterday. We've been friends for more than 30 years. I said I don't know how to break away from this hold mom has on me. It's too much, and it's a burden.

Ellen said she remembered it all really well.

She said, "We spent so much time together growing up. Your grandmother tried to shield you from your mom. It's like she knew something was off. But, then, it became a power play.

Your grandmother was in more control and your mom didn't like it, so she took you out of your private school safe zone and tossed you into public school mid-year.

It was a devastating blow. And, it wasn't the best decision for you, but she needed control."

I was amazed out how much she understood. From two decades ago. I said that's the way I remembered it too, but I was hoping my memory was skewed. I would have been much better off staying in that safe small school house for a couple more years. Those kids and those teachers made me feel safe. And being yanked from it all in a rush was a bit of a trauma.

Mom told me I'd be the "popular kid." And, for about 5 minutes I was.

Some of the kids remembered me from my stint in daycare a few years before, but when the quiet shy girl came out, and I was the only one of my friends not having sex a year later (in the 7th and 8th grades), it made me a bit of a wallflower.

Ellen said, "No. Even as a child, *at the age of six*, I knew your mom was off. Bat-shit crazy off."

But, I said, "It couldn't have been that bad, right? I mean, I feel so guilty."

Ellen said, "Well, that's the guilt control she's always had over you. And, you are the only child she's been able to do that with long-term. She's reaching for straws. And, I'd say your kids should never go back to her house with what you've described."

But, I said, "I get scared of her. I am scared of her rage. I am scared she might just show up and yell at me. I am scared of her actions."

Ellen said, "Yeah, with our parents, sometimes it's hard not to become that child again. It's hard not to feel that way, but you don't have to.

Block her calls. Do what you *have* to do."

I was thinking it wasn't that bad. I mean, she just doesn't listen to me. I get that. I only disobeyed her a few times, and when I did, she struck me with her hand or with a hanger. It was enough to push me down emotionally and physically.

And, as I type this, I feel the stress in my neck and shoulders and body. The therapist said it is "toxic."

I just know there must be a better way.

I have to stick up for my children. I've said what I needed to say. I don't have to be combative. I just say "stop" when she says what she says. I just avoid her ploys for drama when she starts them via text.

Good distractions

My older creative friend Nancy, who is now a California producer, offered more good advice.

Nancy said, "It wasn't you. I had one run in with her, and I won.

Studies show that abusive women are less likely to change. I mean it's so unnatural that some-how it sticks.

Your mom was tough. She was hard to deal with. It was rough! Rough.

And, you didn't have that balance of a mom and a dad. Your dad was distant, right?"

Me: "Well, yeah, sometimes he helped with school projects. He popped in and out of my life but never filled the picture. So, yeah, that one relationship- -mom and I - -pretty much was all I had."

Nancy, "Did she do drugs? Were there drugs?"

Me: "Well, some when I was younger, a bong, and funny circles of hands and grownups acting child-like.

I just remember everything always being up and down. Fear."

Nancy, "Yeah, but that's all you had. So every relationship kind of bounces off of that reflection."

But, I don't remember

It helps to have heard from my friends and to know objectively that growing up was really Hell, and it was not all in my head, but for me, it was my normal. And, to hear that it wasn't normal gave me a new perspective. It also makes me feel weird knowing that my world wasn't everyone else's world.

In trying to be my own person, I also fight not turning in to her- -not turning into all I know.

Losing friends because I treated them the way she treated me, was eye-opening.

I realize pacing is important. I realize being quiet is also important.

I realize not pushing boundaries is important.

New turns. New life.

So where does that girl go? The one who is letting go and making very little if not no contact with her mom? When the girl won't let her mother push her down again? When the girl puts all of the clutter down on paper. It's no longer in her head. She has so much more space now—so many more places for freedom. When that girl gives herself permission to put everything-without holding back-on paper?

When that girl can finally be as strong as she can be, and there's no one to hold her back? What if she stands taller than her mom? What if she is smarter than her mom? What if she is prettier and more kind?

What if it's not pride, but confidence-unyielding?

I tell Nancy how much I love my creative friends, who are "family" to me.

When I realized I was an intuitive soul, it really was a coming-out of sorts. I had found me, and I had found people like me. I wasn't alone.

Nancy said, "It's okay to love your music (family) that much … you don't really have anyone like that. It's okay to follow your heart."

I said, "But it's *embarrassing* to need people."

Nancy said, "It's okay to need people."

Photography

Today I went to the park twice and shot more than 100 photos. I have about 10 that I loved and about 5 of those were a surprise shot.

My friend Tony gave me some pointers, and I went back and took better shots. He said, "go more extreme," and I was really proud of my shots

It's hard to measure growth. But, going more extreme is what I am doing these days with more than photography, with my life.

Mom is a ghost now, and I wonder what she's up to. But, at the same time, I am finding healing, and I love it.

I don't know what to do with this new freedom. I don't know where to go next or how. I don't know if I'll ever really be completely free.

I see her in my hands, in the mirror and in the way I put on my clothes. I see her everywhere and the farther I run, the more her memory chases me. It's very *Glass Menagerie* because the farther I run, the more I realize that escape is only an illusion.

Crap

It was this constant dance. And, I'd lose more and more of me in the process to make more and more of her happy. I was her puppet. And, now to wander from her hand, makes me feel lost, hurt, like a part of me is gone, but also free to figure out how to fill in all of the blank spots. But, it's also hard because I keep looking back for her permission, for her "blessing" even as she doesn't believe in any of that "crap."

I feel her solemn pout.

So, I let go and walk away, and I try to find people that could love me back. And, the odd thing is, I often don't know how to receive that kind of love. If it's not a war, how is it so simple? It's hard not to make it a game of war and stones. I don't trust the fall.

I find treasures in banged up people. I see parts of myself and with them, I feel more whole.

Forward

The therapist said the next step is to move forward honoring myself, it's not about pushing away my mom but honoring myself and in the way I want to be treated.

It's about honoring what I need and making the way for positive relationships to flourish. And she said not to measure it as it has taken so long, but in my own pacing of life, step by step.

I feel like I am on a trapeze, and I'm just swinging upside down- -hoping to grab onto something. My head is filling up, and my face is red, and now I've let my arms go and, I'm just dangling here because my legs have gone numb from the bar beneath my knees.

Blood

I tell my therapist the story about the blood-scattered bathroom dream. He asks if I'm on any medication.

I said, "Nope. In fact, I no longer need even my thyroid meds."

He said, "You are so much more than you believe yourself to be. You've been through so much, and it sounds like Hell."

I ask, "But how do I tell her I need space, time, say anything at all."

He said, "You say you need space, and she needs to respect that."

"Just like that?"

"Just like that, and think about how you could help others like yourself. . . to believe that they can recover from circumstances like your own."

"Yeah."

"Yeah."

With tears in my eyes and his, I leave the therapist's office lighter. I leave the shaking maybe-it-wasn't as bad as I thought thoughts down. I leave with validation. I leave with confidence. I leave taking off the layer of childhood mask over my face and allow myself to be shiny and new and everything I've always wanted to be.

Shining

I wear the pretty black dress. Not to pick up people. Not to make a scene, but because of the way it makes ME feel. I walk into the music scene. It's dark and very quiet. The musician that is always there is singing the same song, looks up and forgets the line in the song. He stumbles and apologizes out loud on the mic.

Inside, I'm laughing.

And, after three years of seeing the same musician over and over, later that night, he finally sees me too. He finally looks me in the eyes and gets why I'm there. I'm finally seen. At my best.

And, later I talk to my creative friend. I tell him I am glad to see him doing something new up on stage. He was alive-electric.

He looks up and smiles and says, "It's good to see you this way too."

And, I left smiling from the inside out.

Therapy

Me to therapist: The thing is, I feel so guilty at times. I want to call, and just give her everything she needs and wants. It's not about me. I just want *her* to be happy.

Therapist: What about *you*?

Me: What about *me*? I am never in the equation.

Therapist: What would she say?

Me: She would say I'm not happy. I act robotic around her. It's some sort of defense mode.

Therapist: Let's role play. I am your mom. 'So why are you mad?'

Me: you hurt me. Your words hurt me. All of the time. A lot of the time.

Therapist: Changing roles. That's all you'd need to say.

Me: I guess I know when I'll be ready to talk to her; I won't shiver when I talk about her. I guess I'll know when it's time.

Therapist: Yes.

Me: These feel like tiny BIG steps.

Therapist: Yes. Truth is, you probably should have done this years ago. But, now was the time for you.

Me: But, it's not easy. It's not easy to think of myself as an adult and not always under someone. Every single relationship I have is impacted by this one.

Therapist: Well, you are way beyond a child at this point. You are nearly forty.

He laughs.

Me: Well, yes, but that's my truth. That is how I struggle to see beyond her thumb . . . and to not be under someone, but to be my own person.

Therapist: But think about the things you can do when you are no longer looking at life that way. You have so many talents. A writer. A teacher. A caregiver.

Me: Yes. I guess I'm like Moses. I always want an Aaron. But, then, I realized too that an Aaron can also get in the way …

Therapist: Yes. There's a lot you *can* do…

Safe places

The thing is, working at an elementary school, you are surrounded by boundaries. Students are told when to sit, how to sit, how to cross their legs, when to stand, when to have soft voices, when to run, how to run and where to stand in the hallways. And, it's a weird place to see them thriving on boundaries.

And to come from a world void of boundaries is a strange place. And to be in this place of establishing boundaries, and safety is a weird place too.

The teachers have safe places. The rooms are structured. Everyone is safe. Everyone is balanced. People are respected.

Places are firm.

And, here, though, emotionally, and inside my head, I am expecting a tornado to arrive at any moment. And as my shoulders and neck adjust to the calm, and my head rearranges from chaos and constant put downs and hurt and the constant feeling of being under everyone around me, I start to see and acknowledge my own abilities. I start to see what I really am and who I really am. I start to see and to believe in what I'm made of.

Instead of having all of these credentials and hiding in my I'm- not-enough way, I begin to believe that I am-already.

Her voice is slowly leaving my head.

I walk in as a new hero to these small people. I deliver guidance, and they look up to me.

They are sweet kind sitting straight souls. And, I almost struggle to stay awake. How can I be so used to so much turmoil that normal and straight feels like a nap?

My counselor once said that people who live in harsh situations growing up get used to the bad and it becomes their normal. And, having to adjust to a peaceful normal is an adjustment.

Bullies

The thing is everything about life is different now. I see bullies all around me, but I don't feel under everyone around me anymore.

I see her when I look in the mirror. I feel her when I put the dishes in the dishwasher. I see her in various places lurking like a ghost that hasn't given up the keys yet.

But, it's a new sort of confidence now. It's a feeling of wholeness. It's a thing of loving myself completely - -not vanity, but yet seeing my full potential for the first time and embracing the full power of it.

And, five months have passed since I talked to my mom. I miss my sister. I miss my step-dad. I miss my brother. I am not allowed to talk to them now, since mom is mad. I have lost everyone.

Not that they've reached out to me either. Mom and sister slip into conversations like mystery ghost trespassers. But, I am more alive than ever. I am lighter because I am not tripping over the big question- -have I made mom happy? Am I allowed to be happy, if she is not happy.

I am an adult for the first time in forty years of living, and I am my own. I dance when I want. Though, she still appears in my dreams. I wake up sweating. I wake up crying. I wake up curled in a ball.

The interesting thing is now I can see the other side. I see a woman in her forties now still traumatized by her mother. And not by more than three slaps, but by harsh memories of the floor always slipping and emotional whippings. I was always afraid to lose her. She was always threatening to abandon me if I didn't do what she wanted. And, when I left, it took months to shed the coat and layers of threatening barriers that hung over me for decades.

I am living and feeling free and discovering the bright light within me. I am starting to see just what I've been capable of *all of this time*.

For years people have told me this, but I never believed I was worth anything. I never believed I was allowed to shine and to fill in this body of purpose.

If I tried to grow, I was clawed down. Within twenty minutes of my last visit with her, I was stabbed at least eight times with mean comments. I was put in my box. Continually.

I know it's Christmas. I know it was my birthday. I know mom's haunting me in my dreams. I know it's still there like an odd-looking shadow in the corner of the room. But, over time, the shadow has less meaning. It has less power over me, and the bright halo radiating from within me grows, and I am far more sure of myself and who I can be and who I want to be as I shed the bangles from my previous story.

And, as my therapist told me, this is long-past due. But, perhaps now was the perfect time. And, perhaps this tiny step was my heroic journey. Perhaps this leap will save my life.

I am just finding that shedding that layer--that trauma has opened a door to a new beginning I never imagined. It's like now, anything is possible. And, I am beginning to believe it.

Bright spots

It's July 4th, and we are driving across town to our old neighborhood. I'm excited because down the street is Leo. My friend leads kids singing favorite American classics. I wave. I am embraced by hugs.

They sing all of the tunes before exiting the truck loaded with karaoke gear.

We talk and cruise the park for hot dogs and laughing over picnic tables with friends new and old. Everyone is clad in stars and stripes.

I catch Leo near the swings. He said, "I don't always write back, but I wanted you to know I have a whole 'you' file. I appreciate you and keep all of your notes (in a special file)." It's a good moment between me and "grumpy."

A few months later, I'm at his son's show up-front. And, I see him in the back. I grin. I'm a fool. Hubby says so too. I can't help it. I don't *care* about the show. My friend's son is on stage, but his father is in the back. And, my coolness is shattered. I lean around the crowd. Looking for him. Then, I give up, and go find him.

He's near the merch table. I have to stand with him. I can tell he's not feeling well. We talk, and soon loudly so much that people stare. We get to be the idiots talking and laughing too loudly. And I love it. I think if they wanna complain they can, this guy created the guy on stage with the show.

I lean over and like in *The Intern* movie, I confess "You're my best friend." Since I moved an hour away, I've missed him. He says, "I love you too."

Later, he does come up front near the back right side of the stage to smile, and he watches his granddaughter sing with his son. I take a photo, and it's all I can do not to join him. He's smiling with such pride.

Time healing some wounds

Some time has passed. I've matured some. Gained some pride. I've realized I do deserve more. Also, I see the tricks- - the manipulation--the things that make one think it's me that's the crazy one. The details are subtle.

Reading through my oldest child's phone, I see a strange message. I see that a stranger has told him "I'm a friend of 'Raymi' (your grandmother), and she told me to tell you she loves you very much."

My son responded with "ok" I suppose between video games and Youtube movies.

The thing is, the "friend" was actually his grandfather. He had pretended to be someone he was not to his own grandson.

She had contrived with my dad to break a boundary. And, why did he have to lie about who he was?

In the day job

I see students every day dealing with overbearing moms. They clean like crazy people to please their moms. They push themselves past childhood to try to appease monsters. And, all along, they wonder what else they can do. They wonder why, and they feel worthless. They can never win. They can never make their mom happy.

I tell them it's not their fault. I tell them it's not them. I tell them parents make mistakes. They are not perfect. I tell them to believe in themselves. I tell them not to drink the bleach, not to mark their arms. I tell them the footprints on their backs are not because they said a curse word or didn't clean fast enough.

And, I see my story right there too. No, she didn't beat me. She didn't make me drink bleach, just think about jumping from a second story building. I thought if I broke my legs, that pain would be better than the emotional pain I was feeling at the time. I thought if I bruised my arms with the firewood, the pain would cover the unloved pain and the constant pain of trying to please someone.

New loves that make me whole

Like my photography, I feel the magic in the artist craft of feeling the story and crafting it out.

The photo and music stories are what keep me alive-what keep me off antidepressants- -what keep me afloat when counseling abused students 2-4 times a week. The photos and writing are what make sense in my life and make me, me.

Texting through walls

A year passed. And, after some time, I was so much better. I had perspective. I had weighty confidence. I had more head on my shoulders.

We agreed to meet with her, and she changed the schedule. She said she's, as usual, all-of-a-sudden busy.

A few weeks pass, I get a call.

I am not able to answer at that time, and she always calls at the exact wrong time.

I waited two hours, and I called back. Already apologizing, I recall.

"We were in swimming lessons when you called…"

And, I went on to babble about swim skills and a job 550 miles from home.

She stops with a whimper and a power play, 'Well, if you're not going through something, call sometime, we are around.'

I said, "Ok." And, I tell my son he can have my phone, and I hang up just after audibly saying those remarks.

Text two

A week passes, and it's all the same again.

I get this text, and I feel the punishment of childhood all over again. My head on the ground at her feet. Below her feet, if I can get that low. I can not be punished enough emotionally. I can never get low enough beneath her.

But, I am stronger now, and though that thin cape is still hanging in the corner of the room, I can resist it now.

The text came later.

I just read it, and I stepped back. She wanted revenge.

"If you ever want a relationship again … I realized I just can't let you slide right back in as if you hadn't called me for two years (it was one year).

I learned so much about you during that time that a one-on-one is probably the only way we have a chance. I guess if having me in your life is worth that time, I will work that out."

She wants me alone, as a child again, at her feet. And, I can't be alone with her. I can't give her that power over me anymore.

I can't burn the cape, but I can ignore it.

More bright moments with music and creativity

It's Christmas time. Three days before the big day. I get out of work early. I am driving 85 miles to sing carols with Leo and a few good friends. It's a magical time.

I see my friend. He shares about his new singing troop. He said it's a little like AA where the group prays and tells stories. He said it's a good group. He's a little behind in the prayer unit. I make a sign of the cross that looks more like a baseball field or an umpire scratching in odd directions. He laughs.

We have small talk over appetizers. He doesn't like the spicy food either. He's fun to do nothing with. I appreciate that trying out foods we don't like together can be an event.

Across the room while I take photos, my 76-year-old best friend winks at me. It makes me laugh.

He says when I bought my camera that "We're gonna have great photos too!"

Outside we carol. He laughs and shares stories and becomes Elvis and then sings "All I want for Christmas is my two ffffront tfffeeth." It's perfect.

The best part is that neither one of us is on. We aren't being anything but ourselves. It's easy.

Answering the Phone

Phone rings. I pondered about declining. I accept. Just bite the bullet. It's New Year's Day.

She's clearly driving and hyper or has drank a lot of coffee.

"I just don't get it. You hurt me. I'm in so much pain I want to die.

And you kept me from your son."

I replied "Yes because I needed space and you kept calling and calling him. Over and over."

"But then you had that affair, and you didn't like the guy enough to stay with him. And you had the DNC.

And then you told people I abused you. That's why all your friends looked at me that way. And I only adored you.

And all those years you called me because you were worried about things. You just needed so much attention. Now you live far away with that weirdo and you're a weird too."

This time, the tables were turned. I suddenly became the therapist. I said, "I hear that you're upset. I never said those things and that affair didn't happen. I did say you picked on me. Where are you hearing these things ?"

"It doesn't matter where I heard it!, she screamed, the affair didn't happen? No DNC?" She roars.

I said, "No, but abdominal surgery. Cancer scare."

"Oh well. I'm still so mad! And well I want 5k for the reconstructive. Surgery. . .Since you deceived me, I want it back in a check. You know my address."

She hung up the phone.

Ten minutes later I miss her call, and I call back.

I think how we just put down $10k for a new house. We saved for almost a year for that. I know at best, I could send $100.00 a month. Especially with me driving so much and working such long hours with very little return in this expensive city.

I speak to my husband, and he says we can't pay her that. And he asked, "if we do that, where does it end? What's the next thing she wants you to pay her back for?"

I get a text a day later. She says she's sorry for being angry.

Five hours later, I text again. Same message "I am sorry. I love you." I turn off my phone.

When Dads Lie

Looking back, it's clear my dad must be the gossip in her ear. They were teen heartthrobs and married at age 18. And he's recently divorced, for a third time. He has been the one to feed her half-truths for the past two years. I'm guessing our faded fake friendship on Facebook led him to assume things that never happened. And, these things led him to make up stories for eager ears.

He said I'd never make it backstage on my own. I'd have to have *special* circumstances to get past barriers. It hurt because I do work hard. I have a journalism degree and a lot of photography training and a heart for helping with the hard stuff. I'm even in the handful that stay late to pick up trash with a smile on my face.

To the man who shows up once every few years or so, to the man who wishes me a happy birthday via text then says "great photo," while saying such untrue words, it's hard to be in your world.

Years of counseling and years of learning to counsel others, demand that I consistently reflect. I have taken the time now to reflect on what I needed- -What I hoped to be - -How to make myself whole. How to spread my wings and shine without feeling disobedience. Shedding the image of myself as just a child. Shedding the co-dependence, the enmeshed fringe, hoping to believe in myself by myself. When I did this, I had to cut off her arm. And, now, because of me, she's wanting to kill herself.

Recovery

Looking back, as I started writing this story, I see I gave myself permission to never share this book, to be free, for the first time, ever, not hold back.

I see places when I could have been more fair to her and more fair myself.

I could have expected less.

And, I feel confused with my knee-jerk reactions that linger. The people behind my car are honking that I won't turn right fast enough.

I hear her yelling in the car, in my head, "People, get your thumb out of your asses! What do you need, an invitation? Drive!" I have to hold back. She's not actually in the car with me.

The time in-between

She hasn't called or contacted me since she voiced her demands.

Now, it's been two years, and I consider sending a photo text every Sunday. It's honestly, the bravest thing I can do at this point.

And, I do miss them. But, I don't know how to do it. I don't know how to go back. I reread this, and I see how much of me has really been impacted. I see how much of me has healed over time. I see how much I have overcome.

I see, too, that I could have made her look better. I still have that need to protect my mom. I still want her to be happy. And, I still want to cover up the past. When I started to write this book, however, I promised to be completely honest- for the good and the bad. I just put it all out there, and I knew it wouldn't always be pretty. My friend Leo did that with his story. And, I admired his honesty so much, that I thought I'd just get started writing- -promising to just write without making anything look perfect. He made it look easy. It was hard to write and even harder to read. But, the validation that came from holding those memories in my hands for the first time. Realizing it was all real and not in my head was a huge growing point for me. And, as I read back about the points of light and creative angels that showed up just when I needed them, I realized I wasn't alone. I was never alone.

I learned I have been through so much trauma. As I have counseled other children through the very same things, I understand their stories first hand. They find escape in cutting themselves, for in that moment, the pain goes away. And, they don't yet understand that it's not their fault.

I now see that emotional abuse is very real. And, even if painted over in memory, it comes out later in actions and behaviors. It can eventually become like an invisible cloak. And, all relationships would revolve around that one that didn't work. I'd bend so far one way, I'd lose my own reflection. Relationships-friendships, romance, work-place boundaries; it all was a mess. For my "normal" wasn't the norm.

I know I wasn't perfect. I always knew she loved me. I always knew that. I look back and needed to feel loved. I needed to be heard. I needed to be loved for me--just as I was. I needed to be the child, and when it was time, I needed to be allowed to be the adult.

We are who we are. I am part of my mom, part of my dad, but more of my own. I love them both, and I always will. I can't miss them when I look in the mirror. I will remember the love there, but I will be whole, first.

I will remember the blessings that came along the way--like strength, and eventually, more confidence.

I will be grateful for the substitute dads that came along the way. For an uncle, related only by ex-marriage, who taught me how to ride a bike, a lot about life on a farm, and a lot about working hard. I will be grateful for a music dad that made guitars, the dads that stepped in to toss balls to me and listen. And, I am grateful for a piano teacher that listened to me late in life and pushed me further. I am grateful for friends that became sisters. I am grateful for my music dad, 39 years older than me that makes me laugh, teaches me how to fight for what I care about, to keep going and to not take people's opinions too seriously. I am grateful for creative friends with intuitive gifts that helped me to see my own gifts. I'll never forget when Donna said, "Don't you know you are amazing to talk to? You have great stories, and you need to share them."

Sitting in a room full of writers and inhaling the magic of Sunday evenings with music everywhere was a coming-out of my own. I realized there were creative people just like me that felt deeply and loved deeply and lived to create life deeply.

Sensitive souls that HAVE to create are this rare breed with gifts that are usually not valued. But, we are a powerful brood. Donna said, "I wish I could gather all of us (intuitive creative souls) in one room. Imagine that?" Donna was there encouraging me to give my positive review to one of my favorite musicians that day. She was there to tell me that I was "a bright light," and that my voice needed to be heard. Through her, too, I realized that my intuition and creativity which made me feel very lonely as a child, was a gift. And, I suddenly no longer felt like I was alone.

In days donating my time to give my creative gifts to serve creative people, I have found myself. I am whole. In writing, in photographs, in simply saying "thank you" or being in that creative sacred place, I am the most me--whole.

Whether caroling with my old friend, listening to a new tune or simply learning to be, I am finally free.

I love seeing me for the first time in forty years. I am beginning to really like who I have become. I love not feeling like I am less. I love being whole. I love my life.

I finally have a voice

This book is dedicated to my husband, my children, my adopted dads, my creative family that gave me wings, and to all of those impacted by borderline personality disorder. I am grateful for the angels that came through to remind me that I have a voice.